Introduction

The Royal Air Force was formally created on 1 April 1918. A hundred years on, it has justly celebrated amid a number of special events. Rather than review the well-known and somewhat obvious aircraft that feature in the history of the RAF, the aim of this book is to offer an alternative insight into what has impacted on the RAF within its first century.

The Royal Air Force was formed towards the end of the First World War and is the world's oldest independent air force. It was formed by merging the Royal Flying Corps (RFC) and the Royal Naval Air Service (RNAS). The RAF's naval aviation branch, the Fleet Air Arm, was founded in 1924 but handed over to the Admiralty on 24 May 1939.

Since its foundation, the RAF has seemingly always been involved in a conflict somewhere, particularly during the interwar years when much effort was expended on policing the Empire. In 1920, the RAF was involved in a conflict in British Somaliland; in 1921 the conflict in Mesopotamia started; in 1925 it was Pink's War in Waziristan; on 23 December 1928 the world's first air evacuation began when the British Legion in Kabul was flown to safety; in 1932 the RAF was involved in psychological and conventional warfare in north-east Iraq; all ahead of the Second World War.

Since the Second World War, it has fought wars and conflicts in Malaya, Korea and the Falklands as well as having been involved in the Gulf War (1991), Kosovo (1999), Afghanistan (2001), Iraq (2003) and the intervention in Libya in 2011.

The RAF describes its mission statement as '... [to provide] an agile, adaptable and capable Air Force that, person for person, is second to none, and makes a decisive air power contribution in support of the UK Defence Mission'. This mission statement is supported by the RAF's definition of 'Air Power' which guides its strategy and is defined as 'the ability to project power from the air and space to influence the behaviour of people or the course of events'.

Looking back, many people will recall Hurricanes and Spitfires standing firm against the invading Luftwaffe, but how many will remember the Chain Home radar system or the key role played by the Fighter Controllers? The parachute and ejector seat saved numerous lives, while permitting many pilots to return to the battle. The Lewis Gun had a major part to play in arming numerous aircraft. Then there was the invention of the gun synchroniser, often known as the Interrupter Mechanism, allowing machine-gun bullets to pass safely through the propeller arc without destroying it. Heavy weapons like the Grand Slam, Tallboy and Highball all played a part – each having been designed to solve a particular problem. Consider too the time when some thought that all aircraft would eventually be pilotless, and missiles would replace them; the Thor missile is included in the images.

In modern times, new weapons have come to the forefront of military aviation and this book includes details of Storm Shadow – the air-launched cruise missile; Brimstone – an air-launched ground attack missile; Paveway laser-guided bombs; and RAPTOR – the reconnaissance pod acquired to operate on the RAF's fleet of Tornado GR.4 aircraft.

Looking back on its first 100 years has been a most interesting and entertaining project but what is the future for the Royal Air Force? It certainly involves supporting ongoing British military operations, the introduction of new aircraft types, greater focus on network enabled capabilities along with the increasing interoperability with members of NATO. It will involve an increased use of unmanned combat aerial vehicles (UCAVs) but may also involve increases in the use of Private Funding Initiatives.

New aircraft expected to join the RAF over the coming years include the Lockheed Martin F-35 Lightning II single-seat, single-engine, fifth generation multirole fighter that is currently under development to provide ground attack, reconnaissance and air defence capabilities – all with a stealth capability. It is anticipated that it will enter service with the RAF in 2020 and is expected to replace the remaining Tornado GR.4 aircraft and has been slated to join Nos 17(R), 617 and 207 squadrons.

The F-35 is expected to operate alongside the Typhoon aircraft, which itself is now expected to remain in service until 2040, ten years longer than was previously planned. In recent years, the Government has invested significant sums in developing the Typhoon's air-to-ground capabilities and the integration of the aircraft to carry both Storm Shadow air-launched cruise missiles and Brimstone air-launched ground attack missiles.

The development of Unmanned Aerial Vehicles (UAVs) seems to continue apace. The Protector programme (previously known as the Scavenger) will supply a next-generation medium-altitude, long-endurance UAV to replace the Reaper, currently in service. Delivery of around twenty of the new ER version (extended range – permitting a duration of up to 40 hours) of the Protector is expected by the end of the decade.

Despite problems with the engine gearboxes, deliveries of the A400M Atlas will continue, with a total of twenty-two aircraft expected to enter RAF service, replacing the older Hercules transport aircraft.

On the Signals Intelligence front, all three Boeing RC-135W River Joint intelligence gathering aircraft are now in service with No. 51 Squadron, known in the RAF as the Air Seeker. The Sentinel will remain in service up to 2025, with the Shadow R.1 remaining until 2030.

Meanwhile, new aircraft are expected in the Maritime Patrol role. The RAF is expected to receive nine Boeing P-8 Poseidon aircraft, which will be based at RAF Lossiemouth by 2025. Two squadrons – Nos 120 and 201 – are expected to operate the new type.

In the training role, a Private Finance Initiative valued at £6 billion is expected to be outsourced to the private sector to cover the RAF's training requirement for the next twenty-five years. New aircraft coming into service include the Grob G120TP, the Beechcraft T-6 Texan II and the Embraer Phenom 100 in the fixed-wing environment, while the Eurocopter H135 and H145 are expected to join the rotary-wing training programme. Meanwhile, replacements have yet to be identified for the Vigilant T.1 and Viking T.1 in the motor-glider and glider roles.

As the title suggests, this is predominantly a picture-led volume. In selecting the images for this book I have often been obliged to choose between quality and originality. I have gone to great lengths to include as many 'new' images as possible. Where a poor-quality image has been used, it is because I decided the interest value of the subject matter has warranted the decision, making it a better choice than a familiar, previously published image. After all, while the archives of the Air Historical Branch are enormous, some of the older, historical images of specific events are somewhat limited – photography 100 years ago was not what it is today! Digital photography is having a massive impact on what is available in recent history. Most people carry a smartphone, usually fitted with a good-quality camera, so in many respects we have all become photographers and are recording our history in much greater detail.

All the images in this book have come from the archives of the Air Historical Branch's amazing archives but wherever possible the source of the image and the name of the photographer have been acknowledged in the caption to each illustration. However, on occasions the widespread practice of copying images may have obscured the true origin of some. This may have led to some image credits in this book being incorrect. If this has occurred, it is completely unintentional and I do apologise.

I have tried to make the captions relatively brief but informative, hopefully allowing the images to do the talking. After all, many of them have a significant historical interest!

RAF in 100 Pictures is part of Amberley Publishing's 'A Pictorial History' series and joins *RAF Transport Command* and *Royal Flying* on the bookshelves. Thankfully, it appears that future titles will be added to this series over the coming years.

I sincerely hope this book enlightens and, more importantly, entertains the reader.

Keith Wilson
Ramsey, Cambridgeshire, June 2018

BUCKINGHAM PALACE

LORD ROTHERMERE. AIR MINISTRY. STRAND.

Today the Royal Air Force, of which you are Minister in Charge, comes into existence as a third arm of the Defences of the Empire.   As General-in-Chief I congratulate you on its birth, and I trust that it may enjoy a vigorous and successful life.

I am confident that the union of the Royal Naval Air Service and the Royal Flying Corps will preserve and foster that esprit de corps which these two separate forces have created by their splendid deeds.

GEORGE R.I.

1st.April 1918.

Congratulations from the King on the Formation of the Royal Air Force on 1 April 1918
A copy of a message from HM King George V to Lord Rothermere, the Minister for Air, to mark the formation of the Royal Air Force on 1 April 1918. (*Crown Copyright/Air Historical Branch image AIR-2-100-A12528*)

Formation of the Women's Royal Air Force (WRAF)

On 1 April 1918, alongside the Royal Air Force, the Women's Royal Air Force was formed. Personnel from the Women's Army Auxiliary Corps and Women's Royal Naval Service were given the choice of transferring to the new service and more than 9,000 decided to join. Here, Air Mechanics of the Women's Royal Air Force (WRAF) were photographed while working on the fuselage and engine of a Royal Aircraft Factory R.E.7 training aircraft in 1918. (*Crown Copyright/Air Historical Branch image X-74828*)

Above: The Lewis Gun

The Lewis Gun was a First World War-era light machine gun of US design that was perfected and mass-produced in the UK. The Lewis Gun has the distinction of being the first machine gun fired from an aircraft when, on 7 June 1912, Captain Charles Chandler of the US Army fired a prototype Lewis Gun from the foot bar of a Wright Model B Flyer. The Lewis Gun was used extensively on both British and French aircraft during the First World War, as either a gunner's weapon or to supplement the more common Vickers Gun. In this image, Captain (later Air Chief Marshal) J. M. Robb was photographed while aligning the sights on his No. 92 Squadron S.E.5a, D372/1, at Tangmere in June 1918. (*Crown Copyright/Air Historical Branch image H-1170*)

Opposite above: New Aircraft Allocated to the New Royal Air Force

The alphanumeric military serial system had been introduced in 1916 for aircraft allocated to both the Royal Naval Air Service (RNAS) and the Royal Flying Corps (RFC). When the RNAS and the RFC merged on 1 April 1918, no change in the serialling system resulted. One of the very first aircraft ordered by and delivered to the new Royal Air Force was a Royal Aircraft Factory R.E.8, serial number E24. (*Crown Copyright/Air Historical Branch image H-1180*)

Opposite below: Airships

Royal Naval Air Service Airship R31 was photographed while being prepared for flight during the First World War, in 1918. The 'R' of the serial relates to it being a Rigid airship. R31 was an R31-class ship, built by Shorts at Bedford on Schütte-Lanz principles and was powered by Rolls-Royce Eagle engines. (*Crown Copyright/Air Historical Branch image H-525*)

Launching Aircraft from a Towed Lighter

The Sopwith 2F-1 Camel was developed essentially for naval use with seaborne forces. When 'real' aircraft carriers were not available, a scheme was devised to launch the aircraft from a flying-off platform towed behind another vessel. The very first lighter test was made on 30 May 1918 when Lt-Col. C. R. Samson took off from lighter H3, being towed behind HMS *Truculent*, in Sopwith Camel N6823. The system was used for real on 11 August 1918 when Lt S. D. Culley was airborne in just 5 feet and climbed to height before shooting at and destroying Zeppelin L53. It was the last German airship shot down during the First World War. This image was taken looking back from HMS *Truculent* to lighter H3, from which the Sopwith Camel had just alighted after a successful trial. (*Crown Copyright/ Air Historical Branch image H-300*)

1,650 lb SN-Type Bomb
The first 1,650 lb 'SN'-Type bomb was dropped on Middelkirke by a Handley Page 0/400 flown by Sgt L. A. Dell of No. 214 Squadron. It represented the largest bomb used by the RFC/RAF during the First World War. In this image, members of No. 207 Squadron pose at Ligescourt with examples of the SN-Type bomb along with the smallest bombs in use in August 1918. (*Crown Copyright/Air Historical Branch image H-2339*)

Interrupter Gear

A gun synchronizer, sometimes referred to as interrupter gear, was attached to the armament of a single-engine tractor-type aircraft to enable it to safely fire through the arc of its spinning propeller without bullets striking the blades. Design of and experimentation with the concept had begun in France and Germany back in 1913–14 although the first practical – if somewhat unreliable – application was that fitted to the Eindecker monoplane fighters, which entered service in mid-1915. By 1917, a reliable hydraulic British Constantinesco gear had become available. One aircraft to benefit from the application of the interrupter gear was the Sopwith Camel F.1 single-seat Scout, seen in this image, which was armed with a pair of Vickers Guns set just a few inches apart and firing through the propeller arc. (*Crown Copyright/Air Historical Branch image H-1009*)

Hucks Starter

The Hucks Starter is an auxiliary power unit, mounted on a vehicle chassis, and is used to start aircraft engines. These mechanical aids replaced a member of the ground crew turning the propeller by hand. As the engines became larger, it became more difficult and dangerous for the ground crew to turn them over to start. In RAF service, they were usually based on Ford Model T trucks and were named after their inventor – Bentfield Hucks – who was a captain in the Royal Flying Corps. The power is transmitted to the aircraft via a power take-off shaft. The shaft of the starter fits into a special protruding hub incorporating a simple projecting claw clutch on the centre of the aircraft's propeller assembly. The Huck Starter came into service with the RAF in the 1920s and 1930s. In this image, an RAF technician prepares to use a Hucks Starter to power up Bristol F.2B Fighter J6611. (*Crown Copyright/Air Historical Branch image H-67*)

No. 1 School of Technical Training

No. 1 School of Technical Training (SoTT) at Halton, Buckinghamshire, is the RAF's aircraft engineering school and was opened back in 1919. The RAF Aircraft Apprentice Scheme was initiated by Lord Trenchard in 1922. In July 1952, No. 1 SoTT received royal recognition when HM Queen Elizabeth II presented the School with a colour. In this image, the Chief of the Air Staff, Air Chief Marshal Sir Hugh Trenchard, was seen inspecting the apprentice airmen of No. 1 Entry on their passing out from No. 1 School of Technical Training at Halton. (*Crown Copyright/Air Historical Branch image H-2463*)

Air Policing over the North-West Frontier of India

The North-West Frontier region of the British Indian Empire was the most difficult area to conquer in South Asia, strategically and militarily. Reformed at Lahore in India from the disbanded No. 97 Squadron RAF on 1 April 1920, No. 60 Squadron, now equipped with Airco DH.10 bombers, began an association with the Middle and Far East that was to last for forty-eight years. Between the wars, the unit found itself involved in many conflicts along the North-West Frontier, including Pink's War, flying both Airco DH.9A and Westland Wapiti general-purpose aircraft until Bristol Blenheim aircraft arrived six months before the start of the Second World War. This image depicts a Westland Wapiti IIA, J9719/N, of No. 60 Squadron operating over the North-West Frontier of India. (*Crown Copyright/ Air Historical Branch image H-1540*)

Formation of the Fleet Air Arm of the RAF

The Fleet Air Arm of the Royal Air Force was formed on 1 April 1924, encompassing those RAF units that normally embarked on aircraft carriers and fighting ships. The aircraft did not come under the direct control of the Admiralty until mid-1939. No. 810 Naval Air Squadron was a Fleet Air Arm carrier-based squadron formed on 3 April 1933. It was initially assigned to the aircraft carrier HMS *Courageous* in May 1933 and formed part of the Home Fleet. Initially equipped with twelve Blackburn Darts, it was re-equipped with Blackburn Baffin aircraft in July 1934. This image shows a Blackburn Baffin carrier-borne torpedo bomber – S1359/523 – in the markings of No. 810 NAS while serving on HMS *Courageous* when it was photographed taking the wire in 1936. (*Crown Copyright/Air Historical Branch image H-52*)

The Aeroplane and Armament Experimental Establishment (A&AEE) at Martlesham Heath
RAF Martlesham Heath was first used as a Royal Flying Corps airfield during the First World War. In 1917, it became home to the Aeroplane Experimental Unit of the RFC, which had moved from Upavon. In 1924, it was renamed the Aeroplane and Armament Experimental Establishment (A&AEE) and evaluated and tested many of the aircraft types that would eventually enter service with the RAF. This image shows an Avro 594 Aldershot I, J6853, which spent most of its service life based at the A&AEE at Martlesham Heath for trials work. (*Crown Copyright/Air Historical Branch image H-848*)

Above: The Parachute

Although the design of the earliest primitive parachute goes back almost 4,000 years, the modern parachute was invented in the later eighteenth century by Louis-Sébastien Lenormand in France. In 1907, Charles Broadwick demonstrated two key advances in the parachute he used when jumping from a hot air balloon at fairs – he folded his parachute into a pack and the parachute was pulled from the pack by a static line. After the First World War, military development of the parachute continued and this image shows a Corporal Dobbs parachuting from Fairey Fawn J7184 *c.* 1926/27, when the aircraft was used for trials at the Home Aircraft Depot, based at RAF Henlow. (*Crown Copyright/Air Historical Branch image H-1200*)

Opposite above: Mobile Wireless Telegraphy Trailer

An example of an RAF Mobile Wireless Telegraphy Trailer in use at RAF Hendon during the Air Pageant held on 10 July 1929. (*Crown Copyright/Air Historical Branch image H-497*)

Opposite below: RAF Fire Tenders

In 1922, the fire training of RAF personnel commenced at RAF Cranwell, where a small unit was established to train a trade known as 'Aircraft Handler/Firefighter'. The unit was controlled by the London Fire Brigade, who also provided the instructors and devised the training methods and schedules. Little is known of the activities and effectiveness of the unit at RAF Cranwell; however, it remained linked with the London Fire Brigade well into the 1940s. In this image, an early Merryweather Fire Tender is being prepared for use at RAF Hendon in July 1929. (*Crown Copyright/ Air Historical Branch image H-498*)

Aircraft Carrier Operations

Following the formation of the Fleet Air Arm of the Royal Air Force, it controlled those aircraft normally embarked on aircraft carriers. In this image, taken aboard HMS *Courageous*, there are a number of Blackburn Baffin aircraft. Serial numbers identified from this image include K3552/75, K3555/70 and S1558/62. The presence of S1558 aboard would indicate that this image was taken in the late 1920s. (*Crown Copyright/Air Historical Branch image H-824*)

Fairey Long-Range Monoplanes

The Fairey Long-range Monoplanes were a pair of British experimental aircraft designed in the late 1920s and early 1930s. The first aircraft (J9479) was designed to meet Air Ministry Specification 33/27, for an aircraft to beat the absolute distance world flying records. It made its first flight from Northolt on 14 November 1928 and its first attempted record was a trip to Bangalore, India. It failed to break the record on 16 December 1929 but, sadly, it crashed in Tunis, killing the crew and destroying the aircraft. A second aircraft (K1991) was ordered and later made a world record flight to Walvis Bay, South Africa – a distance of 5,410 miles. Later, with no further long-range record attempts planned, K1991 was scrapped. This image shows the first aircraft – J9479 – in flight during its test programme shortly after delivery to the RAF on 7 December 1928. (*Crown Copyright/Air Historical Branch image AHB-MIS-HF-7996*)

High-Altitude Record Aircraft

The Bristol Type 138 High Altitude Record Aeroplane was developed and produced by the Bristol Aircraft Company in the 1930s. From the outset it was designed as a dedicated research aircraft capable of reaching high altitudes. It holds the distinction of setting nine separate altitude world records, the ultimate of these occurring on 30 June 1937 during a 2¼-hour flight flown by Flight Lieutenant M. J. Adam, in which he achieved a record altitude of 53,937 ft (16,440 m) during a flight from Farnborough. The pilot wore a special Siebe-Gorman high-altitude suit for the record attempts. In this image is the Bristol Type 138A high-altitude research aircraft, K4879, which was built to Specification 2/34. (*Crown Copyright/Air Historical Branch image H-1695*)

Autogyros

The Cierva C-30A was built under licence by Avro and supplied to the RAF as the Avro Type 671 Rota 1. Twelve were supplied to the RAF and delivered from August 1934 to May 1935. Initially, these served with the School of Army Co-operation at Old Sarum pre-war, then with No. 1448 (Radar Calibration) Flight at Duxford from 1940, before being delivered to No. 529 Squadron at RAF Halton – becoming the RAF's only autogyro squadron until being disbanded in October 1945. In this image, an Avro Type 671 Rota I, possibly K4239 of No. 5 Radio Maintenance Unit Calibration Flight, was photographed while being wheeled into position by groundcrew at Duxford, Cambridgeshire, ahead of a flight. (*Crown Copyright/Air Historical Branch image CH-1426*)

Approved
E R I

College of Arms,
October, 1936.

Chester Herald
and Inspector of Royal
Air Force Badges.

Squadron Badges and Heraldry

The badge of No. 70 Squadron. It was among the very first to have been officially approved, in October 1936; the circlet features – as was customary at the time – the role of the unit and the squadron number in roman numerals. Until very recently, the colours used for the paintings were not standardized and that of No. 70 features a much darker blue than others painted subsequently. Also of note is the signature of HM King Edward VIII approving the design, 'E RI' translating as 'Edward, King and Emperor' in Latin (*Rex* and *Imperator*). (*Crown Copyright/ Air Historical Branch image AHB-BADGE-SQUADRON-070-ORIGINAL*)

Chain Home Radar

Chain Home (CH) was the codename for the ring of coastal early warning radar stations built by the RAF before and during the start of the Second World War to detect and track enemy aircraft. The radar equipment itself was given the name Air Ministry Experimental Station Type 1 (AMES Type 1) in 1940. Chain Home was the first early warning radar network in the world, and the first military radar system to reach operational status. Its impact on the outcome of the Second World War, particularly in the defence of the UK during the Battle of Britain, cannot be understated. This image shows the AMES Type 1 CH East Coast radar installation at Poling, West Sussex. On the left are three (originally four) in-line 360-foot steel transmitter towers, between which the transmitter aerials were slung, with the heavily protected transmitter building in front. On the right are four 240-foot wooden receiver towers placed in rhombic formation, with the receiver building in the middle. (*Crown Copyright/Air Historical Branch image CH-15173*)

Above: **Battle of Britain Sector Operations Room**
Following the building and commissioning of the first five Chain Home stations in 1937, all of which began full-time operations in 1938, a method of controlling the information was required. This led to the formation of the first integrated ground-controlled interception network – the Dowding system – which collected and filtered the information. This image shows No. 11 Group's Operations Room; now known as the 'Battle of Britain Bunker'. Below the clock is the main tote board showing the status of the various airfields and their squadrons. (*Crown Copyright/Air Historical Branch image AIR-16-880-1-4*)

Opposite above: **RAF Armoured Vehicles**
Both the Army and Royal Air Force had access to a significant variety and quantity of armoured vehicles during the Second World War – everything from tankettes to armoured cars, self-propelled artillery and infantry tanks. However, most, if not all, of this equipment was deployed in theatre, leaving home defences a little exposed. However, innovation was not in short supply and a variety of defensive vehicles were converted for home defence use. Here, three locally modified armoured vehicles that were used for airfield defence at the Bomber Command station at RAF Wyton, Cambridgeshire, in July 1940 are pictured. (*Crown Copyright/Air Historical Branch image CH-727*)

Opposite below: **Geodetic Aircraft Construction**
The Wellington bomber, known to many as the 'Wimpy', could fairly claim to be the backbone of Bomber Command's night raids over Germany for a long period of the war, before four-engine bombers took over the task. At one time, during the winter of 1941/42, there were no fewer than twenty-one squadrons of Wellingtons operational with Bomber Command. Chiefly by virtue of its ingenious geodetic lattice-work construction, the Wellington was immensely strong and could sustain significant damage from flak and still return safely home. In this image showing the geodetic structure to very good effect, civilian female workers were photographed assembling Wellington bombers at the Vickers-Armstrong factory in Chester during June 1942. (*Crown Copyright/Air Historical Branch image CH-5975*)

26

Support of Flight Operations

The air and ground crews responsible for the maintenance, servicing and flying of a single Short Stirling B.I of No. 218 Squadron at RAF Marham. Standing at the front are the aircrew: captain, second pilot, flight engineer, observer (navigator), wireless operator, air gunner/bomb aimer and two air gunners. Behind them stand the meteorological officer, a WAAF parachute packer and the Flying Control officer. In the third rank stand twelve flight maintenance crew and eighteen ground servicing crew, and behind them the tractor driver with his bomb-train in front of the eleven-strong 'bombing-up' team. Behind the aircraft to the left is the refuelling team of three airmen with their petrol bowser, and finally, to the right, the oil bowser and its driver. (*Crown Copyright/Air Historical Branch image CH-5988*)

Wellington Directional Wireless Installation (DWI)

A Vickers Wellington DWI (Directional Wireless Installation) II of No. 1 General Reconnaissance Unit at Ismailia, Egypt, showing the 48-foot diameter electromagnetic ring for exploding magnetic mines suspended from the wings and fuselage of the aircraft. On 8 January 1940, a Wellington equipped with a DWI successfully exploded a mine near the Tongue lightship, north of Margate, the very first success for this anti-mining operation. (*Crown Copyright/Air Historical Branch image CM-5315*)

Above: Tactical Air Force
The term 'tactical air force' was used by the Royal Air Force during the latter stages of the Second World War, to identify formations of more than one fighter group. A tactical air force was intended to achieve air supremacy and perform ground attack missions and was particularly effective in the Western Desert. Here, a pilot of No. 274 Squadron taxies out in his Hawker Hurricane I during a practice scramble at Amriya, Egypt. (*Crown Copyright/Air Historical Branch image CM-128*)

Opposite above: Pickett-Hamilton Retractable Fort
The open spaces of airfields were particularly vulnerable to attack by airborne troops and it was of significant importance to defend them effectively. One such solution was the Pickett-Hamilton retractable fort, a type of hardened field fortification built in Britain during the invasion crisis of 1940–41. It was designed to be lowered into the ground while not in use and as such would be inconspicuous. The fort could be raised by around 2 feet 6 inches above ground, from where a small crew could fire with rifles or light machine guns. This photograph shows the Pickett-Hamilton fort at RAF Tangmere and was taken on 8 June 1941. (*Crown Copyright/Air Historical Branch image CH-17936*)

Opposite below: Aircraft Impressed into RAF Service
Armstrong Whitworth AW.15 Atalanta DG454 was photographed at Ambala, India. This aircraft was impressed into RAF service from Indian Transcontinental Airways and was used to fly reinforcements into Iraq during Raschid Ali's revolt in 1941. DG454 was one of five Atalanta aircraft impressed into service in 1941 and had previously operated as G-ABTM. (*Crown Copyright/Air Historical Branch image H-624*)

30

PILOTS CLEAR VISION PANEL
AND AREA SIGHT

GUN DOORS SHUT

GUNNERS CLEAR VISION PANEL
AND G.J.3 SIGHT

Fighter Interceptor Unit (FIU)

The Fighter Interceptor Unit (FIU) was a special fighter interceptor unit of the RAF during the Second World War. It was formed at RAF Tangmere in April 1940 with a strength of five Blenheim aircraft. On the night of 22/23 July 1940, the unit achieved the very first airborne radar intercept kill when a Blenheim 1F successfully shot down a Dornier Do-17Z, which crashed into the sea. In addition to its operational duties, the FIU undertook the testing of various equipment and armament. This image is of Havoc I BD126, which was tested by the unit, and forms part of a report on the installation of six .303-inch Browning machine guns into the aircraft. The guns were located just behind the pilot's cockpit, in an enclosed area when not in use, with the weapons designed to fire upwards and forwards. The gunner sat in the nose of the aircraft and fired the weapons remotely. Despite the success of the evaluation programme, the Havoc I was considered too slow for the AI role and the programme was terminated. (*Crown Copyright/Air Historical Branch image AIR-29-28-87-A-1*)

Empire Air Training Scheme

The first RAF aircrew commenced training at No. 25 Elementary Flying Training School (EFTS) at Belvedere, near Salisbury, Southern Rhodesia, in 1940. The scheme had stemmed from a bilateral agreement to form the Rhodesian Air Training Group (RATG). This had received Air Ministry support and was funded by a UK Treasury promise to pay later. No. 25 EFTS was the very first Empire Air Training Scheme to be implemented. Eventually, ten RATG air stations were established and trained more than 10,000 aircrew; of which around 7,600 were pilots. In this image, taken at Belvedere Airport, Salisbury, in 1941, student pilots walk past their de Havilland Tiger Moth training aircraft at No. 25 Elementary Flying Training School (Southern Rhodesia). (*Crown Copyright/Air Historical Branch image CM-1173*)

Above: Merchant Ship Fighter Unit (MSFU)

The Merchant Ship Fighter Unit was an RAF operational aircraft unit based at RAF Speke during the Second World War. The role of the MSFU was to provide pilots, crews, support personnel and aircraft to operate from thirty-five merchant ships outfitted with a catapult on the bow, referred to as Catapult Aircraft Merchant ships (CAM ships), to provide air support to conveys out of reach of land in the early part of the war, particularly when aircraft carriers were scarce. In this image, a Hawker Hurricane I, serial P3620/KE-L, of the Merchant Ship Fighter Unit is being positioned onto its launch trolley on the catapult fitted to a CAM ship at Gibraltar in March 1942. (*Crown Copyright/Air Historical Branch image CH-6918*)

Opposite: Night Fighters and Airborne Interception Radar (AI)

Airborne Interception Radar (AI) was used by the British forces to equip aircraft in the air-to-air role. AI was primarily used by night fighter and interceptor aircraft of the RAF and FAA for locating and tracking other aircraft. AI was first used around 1936, when a group at Bawdsey Manor Research Centre began examining how such a radar set could be installed into an aircraft. The development led to the Airborne Interception Mk IV, the very first production air-to-air radar, which entered service in 1940. Commencing with AI Mk VII, AI moved to microwave frequencies utilising the cavity magnetron and greatly improved performance while reducing both weight and size. This image shows the Air Interception Radar type AI Mk VIIIb indicator and receiver in the operating position as seen from the observer's seat of a de Havilland Mosquito NF.XIII night fighter. The visor has been removed from the screen on the indicator unit (top). The receiver unit (bottom) was hinged to allow it to be stored in the space below the indicator to enable the crew to enter and exit the cockpit via the door at the front right. (*Crown Copyright/Air Historical Branch image CH-16606*)

Above: Air-Sea Rescue

The Marine Branch of the RAF was formed back in 1918, just days after the RAF, and operated watercraft in support of RAF operations. During the Second World War they were particularly effective in rescue operations, especially when operating their high-speed launches (HSL). On 6 February 1941, the Air Sea Rescue Services (ASRS) were created, which later became the RAF Search and Rescue Force. In addition to the HSLs, a number of aircraft were used in the air-sea rescue role and the teamwork between air and water-based assets saved many lives. In this image taken during a search on 25 October 1942, a Vickers Wellington IC, 'X' of the Sea Rescue Flight based at LG 'X'/Abu Sueir North, Egypt, was photographed while flying over the Mediterranean Sea, accompanied by an RAF high-speed rescue launch. (*Crown Copyright/Air Historical Branch image CM-3685*)

Opposite: Temperature and Humidity (THUM) Flight

During the Second World War, the weather had a significant impact on RAF operations. As a consequence, an RAF Flight equipped initially with Spitfire and Boston aircraft was set up at Boscombe Down in 1942, to investigate meteorological problems associated with the wartime operations of aircraft. In addition, the Temperature and Humidity Flight (THUM) was also set up and operated from RAF Bircham Newton in Norfolk. In this image, a ground crewman hands a psychrometer to meteorological pilot Flying Officer J. B. Gordon of No. 521 Squadron in Gloster Gladiator II N5897/E before he departs on a high-altitude THUM (Temperature and Humidity) flight from Bircham Newton on 16 January 1943. (*Crown Copyright/Air Historical Branch image CH-18063*)

Above: **Airborne Lifeboats**
Airborne Lifeboats were powered lifeboats made to drop from fixed-wing aircraft into water to aid in air-sea rescue operations. These airborne lifeboats were dropped by parachutes from the underside of heavy bomber aircraft – including Wellington and Lancaster aircraft. In this image, an airborne lifeboat is parachuted by a Lockheed Hudson of No. 279 Squadron to the crew of a US Army Air Force B-17 Flying Fortress who had difficulty getting into their dinghy after making a forced landing in the North Sea on 25 July 1943. At the time of the image, No. 279 Squadron was based at RAF Bircham Newton in Norfolk. (*Crown Copyright/Air Historical Branch image C-3691*)

Opposite above: **British Commonwealth Air Training Plan (BCATP)**
The BCATP was a major programme for training Allied air crews during the Second World War that was administered by the Canadian Government and commanded by the Royal Canadian Air Force (RCAF). Schools and facilities were set up at 231 locations across Canada, many of which were airfields. The BCATP remains one of the largest aviation training programmes in history and was responsible for training almost half of the pilots, navigators, bomb aimers, air gunners, wireless operators and flight engineers who served with the RAF, FAA, RAAF, RCAF and RNZAF. Similar facilities were operated in South Africa, where a further 33,347 aircrew were trained. In this image, student RAF pilots in three Harvard aircraft were photographed while flying over the snowy Canadian landscape during training in March 1943. (*Crown Copyright/Air Historical Branch image CAN-2317*)

Opposite below: **Photographic Reconnaissance**
A de Havilland Mosquito PR.XVI, NS502/M, of No. 544 Squadron, in flight from RAF Benson in December 1944, complete with the D-Day recognition stripes. The under-fuselage camera ports are evident in this photograph of the aircraft as it banks away. The arrangement shows a typical fit for high-altitude reconnaissance, consisting of a vertical 'split pair' of F24 (14-inch) cameras in the bomb bay, a further 'split pair' of F52s (20- or 36-inch) further along the centreline with a single, port-facing oblique F24 in between. It is quite likely that the wartime censor deleted various 'sensitive' aerials from this image. (*Crown Copyright/Air Historical Branch image CH-14263*)

Above: 'Highball' Bouncing Bomb

After having achieved such success with the original 'Upkeep' bouncing bomb against the German dams during Operation Chastise in May 1943, inventor Barnes Wallis went on to develop the 'Highball' weapon which he saw as being 'essentially for the Fleet Air Arm'. It was conceived as a method of dealing with the German battlecruiser *Tirpitz*, which was moored at Trondheim. After some initial testing at Chesil Beach and Reculver, three specially modified Mosquito B.4 aircraft dropped inert weapons in Loch Striven against the former French battleship *Courbet*. Later trials, once again in Loch Striven, were mounted against the old battleship HMS *Malaya*, then held in reserve. Despite the successes during the trials, 'Highball' was never used operationally. This image is believed to have been taken during the trials against HMS *Malaya* in Loch Striven in May 1944 when modified Mosquito B.4 aircraft 'attacked' the vessel, during which time one inert weapon struck the vessel and punched a hole in her side. (*Crown Copyright/Air Historical Branch image ADM-277-46-028*)

Opposite: Airborne Propaganda Leaflets

Airborne leaflet propaganda was a form of psychological warfare in which leaflets were dropped from aircraft in an attempt to change the behaviour in enemy-controlled territory or, on occasions, to warn them of an impending operation. This is Air Ministry Propaganda Leaflet number EH(S)210 – with the slogan 'Courage Belgian friends! England is fighting to deliver you. She will win!' (*Crown Copyright/ Air Historical Branch image AM-PropagandaLeaflet-EHS210*)

Courage, amis belges!

L'Angleterre se bat
pour vous délivrer

ELLE VAINCRA!

Courage, amis belges!

L'Angleterre se bat
pour vous délivrer

ELLE VAINCRA!

ZEGEVIEREN!
HET ZAL
OM U TE VERLOSSEN
ENGELAND STRIJDT
Belgische vrienden,
houdt moed!

ZEGEVIEREN!
HET ZAL
OM U TE VERLOSSEN
ENGELAND STRIJDT
Belgische vrienden,
houdt moed!

Above: Servicing Commando Units

The Royal Air Force Commandos were formed in 1942 from units of the RAF and served in the European and Far Eastern theatres of the war, before being disbanded in 1946. These units, called Servicing Commandos, would accompany the Allied armies when they invaded Europe, either to make German airfields serviceable or to construct new airstrips built by the Army Airfield Construction Unit. The force consisted of 2,400 officers and men skilled in aircraft maintenance, armaments, communications and airfield activation skills. They were capable of working on all types of aircraft to keep them flying under all conditions. This image, taken at B2/Bazenville, Normandy, on 15 June 1944, shows members of the Servicing Commandos loading 3-inch rocket projectiles onto a Hawker Typhoon IB of No. 247 Squadron. (*Crown Copyright/Air Historical Branch image CL-157*)

Opposite: Barrage Balloons

The barrage balloon is a large kite balloon used to defend against aircraft attack by raising aloft cables which posed a serious risk of collision. Some of the barrage balloons also carried small explosive charges that, in the event of contact with the cables by aircraft, would be pulled up against the aircraft to ensure its destruction. This image, taken over 'King' Beach, Gold Sector, on the afternoon of D-Day, 6 June 1944, shows the effectiveness of a low-flying protective balloon barrage manned by RAF balloon teams. (*Crown Copyright/Air Historical Branch image CL-42*)

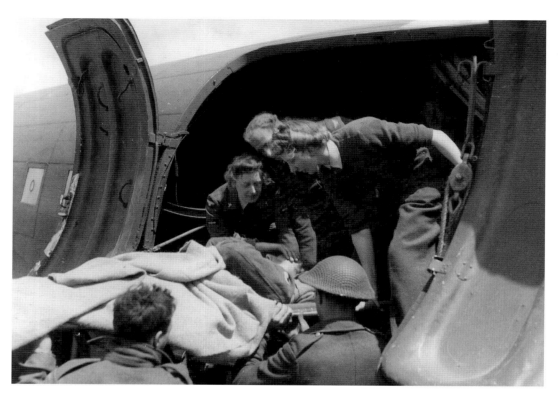

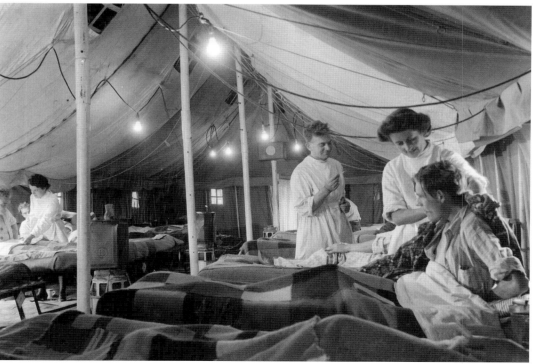

44

Above: Anti-Aircraft Guns

Five gunners of No. 1307 Wing clean their 20 mm Hispano light anti-aircraft gun at Meiktila airfield, Burma, in February 1945, while a motorcycle rider looks on. From left to right: Flying Officer H. E. Cooper, Leading Aircraftsmen W. Bevan, K. Abbott, W. Collins and J. McInally with Corporal Roy Adams. In the background is a Stinson L-5 liaison aircraft of No. 194 Squadron, the only aircraft capable of landing at the airfield during the three-week siege by the Japanese in March 1945, when the aircraft was used for casualty evacuation. (*Crown Copyright/Air Historical Branch image CF-342*)

Opposite above: RAF Flight Nurses – the 'Flying Nightingales'

Nursing orderlies of the WAAF flew on RAF transport aircraft to evacuate the wounded from the Normandy battlefields. They were nicknamed 'Flying Nightingales' by the press. In this image, a casualty is lifted onto a Dakota for repatriation to the UK from France in June 1944. (*Crown Copyright/ Air Historical Branch image CL-173*)

Opposite below: Mobile Field Hospitals

A field hospital is a small mobile medical unit that temporarily takes care of casualties on-site before they can be safely transported to more permanent facilities. This image shows the interior of one of the tented wards at No. 50 Mobile Field Hospital in Normandy, July 1944. Sister M. Griffiths helps one of the patients into his dressing gown. (*Crown Copyright/Air Historical Branch image CL-310*)

Above: 'Grand Slam'

The Grand Slam was a 22,000 lb (10,000 kg) earthquake bomb used by RAF Bomber Command against strategic targets during the Second World War. Designed by Barnes Wallis, it was known officially as the 'Bomb, Medium Capacity, 22,000 lb' and was a scaled-up version of the Tallboy bomb. In this image, a 22,000 lb Medium Capacity high-explosive deep penetration bomb is manoeuvred onto a trolley by crane in the bomb dump at RAF Woodhall Spa for an evening raid by No. 617 Squadron on the railway bridge at Nienburg, Germany, on 22 March 1945. Twenty aircraft took part in the raid and the target was successfully destroyed. (*Crown Copyright/Air Historical Branch image CH-15369*)

Opposite: Mail Flights

A lesser-known but nevertheless essential role of Transport Command during the Second World War was the moving of mail, particularly to the front line, providing a significant boost of morale to those soldiers serving there. In this image, Sergeant H. Stillwell unloads mail bags from a Hawker Hurricane IIC of No. 1697 (Air Despatch and Delivery Service) Flight at B2/Bazenville after a mail flight from RAF Northolt. The pilot, Flight Lieutenant W. V. Melbourne, looks on from the cockpit of the Hurricane. (*Crown Copyright/Air Historical Branch image CL-371*)

FIDO

Fog Investigation and Dispersal Operation (FIDO) was a system used for dispersing fog from an airfield. The device was developed by Arthur Hartley for use at RAF bomber stations, permitting the landing of aircraft returning from raids over Germany in poor visibility by burning fuel in rows on either side of the runway. In this image, taken at Graveley on 28 May 1945, an Avro Lancaster of No. 35 Squadron takes off while the FIDO (Fog Investigation and Dispersal Operations) petrol burners are lit on either side of the station's main runway. (*Crown Copyright/Air Historical Branch image CH-15272*)

First Transatlantic Crossing by a Jet Aircraft

When the powers that be decided an RAF formation display team would perform in Canada and the USA in 1948, it created a raft of logistical problems for the participants. Supporting the six Vampire F.3 aircraft were three Mosquito aircraft: one would act as the convoy leader and as the navigator; the second would shepherd the Vampires and act as back-up navigator; while the third would provide meteorological information. In addition three Avro York aircraft provided the transport capabilities. All aircraft arrived safely and the team – led by No. 54 Squadron – performed in both Canada and the USA before returning to the UK. This image, taken at Meeks Field, Iceland, on 12 July 1948 during the outward flight shows six Vampire F.3 aircraft of No. 54 Squadron which performed the first transatlantic crossing by jet aircraft. In addition, one of the Avro York transport aircraft can also be seen. (*Crown Copyright/Air Historical Branch image CHP-977*)

Boulton Paul P.111 Delta-Wing Research Aircraft
The Boulton Paul P.111 delta-wing research aircraft, VT935, pictured during a test flight from Boscombe Down in 1951. Over the three years of the programme, the P.111 suffered a number of relatively minor mishaps and the substantially modified aircraft was re-christened the P.111A. The aircraft's final flight was on 20 June 1958. The airframe is now exhibited at the Midland Air Museum, Coventry. (*Crown Copyright/Air Historical Branch image PRB-1-2473*)

Aries III Flights Over the North Pole

In July 1951, a crew from the Royal Air Force Flying College at RAF Manby made a pair of long-range navigation flights in a specially modified Avro Lincoln B.2, RE367, named *Aries III*. The first was from Keflavik, Iceland, to Eielson Air Force Base in Alaska over the Geographic North Pole. The return flight from Alaska to RAF Manby took them over the Magnetic North Pole. The modified Lincoln B.2 was fitted with the nose of a Lancastrian (sometimes referred to as a Lincolnian), and was the third of five Aries aircraft used by the RAF on a series of long-range navigation flights. In this image, the crew of RE367 *Aries III* pose with their aircraft at RAF Manby after flying over the Geographic North Pole in July 1951. Pictured second from left is the Lincoln's co-pilot, Wing Commander A. H. Humphrey, who was later Marshal of the Royal Air Force, Chief of the Air Staff between 1974 and 1976 and Chief of the Defence Staff from October 1976 to January 1977. (*Crown Copyright/Air Historical Branch image PRB-1-3012*)

51

Above: Helicopter Operations

A Dragonfly helicopter of the Far East Air Force Casualty Evacuation Flight photographed in a jungle clearing at the village of Kampong Termingor in North Perak, Malaya, with a casualty in a pannier basket about to be loaded aboard, to be flown to the hospital at Ipoh. A sitting casualty can be seen already inside the aircraft. Both casualties were Malay kampong guards who had been injured during an attack on their village by terrorists in November 1952. The initial Air Casualty Evacuation trials had been conducted utilising three Dragonfly helicopters of the Far East Air Force in Malaya between 1950 and 1952. Despite the somewhat limited power of the Dragonfly, the trials were deemed a success and paved the way for future RAF helicopter operations in a multitude of applications, but especially in the casualty evacuation role. (*Crown Copyright/Air Historical Branch image CFP-668*)

Opposite above: Swept Wing Development Aircraft

During the 1953 SBAC Show at Farnborough, Avro took the opportunity to highlight its delta wing aircraft programme by flying the first two Vulcan prototypes – VX777 with VX770 behind – in formation with four of the half-scale Avro 707 aerodynamic research aircraft – two Type 707As (WD280 and WZ736) along with one each of the 707B (VX790) and 707C (WZ744). (*Crown Copyright/ Air Historical Branch image PRB-1-6865*)

Opposite below: SAR Helicopters

The Sycamore was the first British-designed helicopter to go into service with the RAF at home and overseas. In this image, Bristol Sycamore HR.14 XG501 of No. 275 Squadron, based at RAF Thornaby, takes off after participating in a search and rescue demonstration at Flamborough Head on 4 August 1955. XG501 joined the squadron in April 1955 but was written off on 15 December 1955 when the tail rotor struck a mast on the Bell Rock Lighthouse and it fell onto the rocks below. (*Crown Copyright/Air Historical Branch image PRB-1-10246*)

Prone Pilot Meteor

Gloster Meteor F.8 WK935 was modified to accommodate a second pilot in the prone position for trials with the Institute of Aviation Medicine at Farnborough and was photographed during a test flight on 2 May 1955. The second pilot rested on a rubber couch with arm and chin rests and controlled the aircraft using a side-stick and hanging pedals operated by moving his ankles. To counter-balance this extra length and weight, WK935 was fitted with the tail section from an NF.12 and the flying controls were power-boosted. A total of ninety-nine flights were carried out before the project was ended and the aircraft was placed in store in April 1956. It was subsequently preserved at the RAF Museum's Cosford site. (*Crown Copyright/Air Historical Branch image PRB-1-9574*)

The Sparrows – the Central Flying School's Formation Display Team
The Central Flying School (CFS) was formed at Upavon, Wiltshire, in May 1912 and is acknowledged as the world's oldest military training establishment. Its initial purpose was to train pilots for the naval and military wings of the Royal Flying Corps but in March 1920 the school began to train instructors for RAF Flying Training Schools. In July 1920, the first CFS team appeared at the Royal Tournament at Hendon in front of an estimated crowd of 40,000 people, who were entertained by the formation flying and aerobatics of five Sopwith Snipe aircraft. Since then, the CFS has been actively involved in providing members of the Air Force and the public alike with displays of formation aerobatics. The Central Flying School's formation display team, the Sparrows, operated four Provost T.1 aircraft from their base at Little Rissington, where they were photographed on 2 July 1957. The team consisted of (L–R) Flt Lts Les Howes, Charlie Kingsbury, (leader) Mike Bradley and Bert Lane, with Flt Lt Wally Black as the nominated reserve. (*Crown Copyright/Air Historical Branch image PRB-1-13518*)

Above: Creation of 'The Memorial Flight'
On 11 July 1957, the RAF's last three Spitfire PR.XIX aircraft from the former THUM (Temperature and Humidity) Flight at RAF Woodvale – PM631, PS853 and PS915 – were flown from Duxford to Biggin Hill to mark the creation of 'The Memorial Flight', which would later become the 'RAF Battle of Britain Memorial Flight'. To mark the occasion, a presentation speech was made by the Air Officer Commanding-in-Chief Fighter Command, AM Sir Thomas Pike. In this rare colour image taken at Biggin Hill on 11 July 1957, a line-up of aircraft was proudly displayed for the opening ceremony. For the flights from Duxford to Biggin Hill, the aircraft were flown by Gp Capt J. E. 'Johnnie' Johnson DSO DFC in PS853, Gp Capt James Rankin DSO in PM631 and Wg Cdr Peter Thompson in PS915. After landing at Biggin Hill, the Spitfires were joined by the last Hawker Hurricane, LF363, as well as Javelins of No. 46 Squadron and Hunters of No. 41 Squadron. (*Crown Copyright/Air Historical Branch image T-301*)

Opposite above: V Force
The V-Bomber force of Valiant, Vulcan and Victor were all in service with the RAF by 1957. The Vickers Valiant had entered service in 1955 with both the B.1 (bomber) and B(PR).1 (strategic reconnaissance) versions; the Avro Vulcan B.1 began to enter service in 1956; while the Handley Page Victor had started to enter service with No. 232 OCU in November 1957 and with No. 10 Squadron at RAF Cottesmore in April 1958. This image, taken on 13 January 1958, features Vulcan B.1A XA904, Valiant BK.1 XD869 and Victor B.1 XA931. (*Crown Copyright/Air Historical Branch image T-532*)

Opposite below: Air-to-Air Refuelling – A Force Multiplier
While air-to-air refuelling had been trialled by a number of organisations, including the trials conducted by Flight Refuelling Limited, in the late 1950s it was further developed by the RAF as a means of extending the range of both its bombers and fighters. Following successful trials, the Vickers Valiant became the RAF's standard tanker until the mid-1960s. In this image, shot on 12 February 1958, two Valiant B(PR)K.1a aircraft – WZ376 and WZ390 – were used for trials by Vickers-Armstrong. Note the cutaway bomb bay and rear fuselage of the refuelling aircraft (WZ376) to accommodate the hose drum unit (HDU or 'Hoodoo') and the air-to-air refuelling hose and drogue. (*Crown Copyright/Air Historical Branch image PRB-1-14665*)

56

No. 111 Squadron Rolls Twenty-Two Aircraft in Formation
Having looped and rolled sixteen Hunter F.6 fighters in formation at the 1957 SBAC Show at Farnborough, No. 111 Squadron decided to go six better for the following year's event and repeat the feat with twenty-two aircraft. In this image, the squadron is seen rehearsing for the air show and the additional aircraft (borrowed from other front line squadrons) required to achieve this spectacular formation are easily recognisable as they had not been painted into the famous all-black colours used by 'Treble One' at this time. (*Crown Copyright/Air Historical Branch image PRB-1-15707*)

Thor IRBM

The Thor Intermediate-Range Ballistic Missile (IRBM) was in service with twenty RAF Squadrons around the UK, each equipped with three missiles and the necessary launching equipment. The then Prime Minister – Harold Wilson – had agreed to the basing of the missiles in the UK as long as they remained under British control. However, they were still 'owned' by the US, which also retained control of the warheads. As a consequence, no effective launch could be made without the agreement of both parties. Thor was always going to be an intermediate solution to a long-term problem, and after having arrived in the UK in September 1958, the dismantling of the missiles and their launch sites began in 1962, when the missiles were returned to the US. (*Crown Copyright/Air Historical Branch image T-2612*)

Bloodhound Surface-to-Air Missiles
Vickers Valiant B(PR)K.1 WZ390 is pictured while being towed at RAF Marham on 29 May 1961. In the background are Bristol Bloodhound surface-to-air missiles of No. 242 Squadron, one of a number of batteries located in East Anglia and Lincolnshire to protect the vital bomber and Thor missile bases from potential attack by Soviet bombers. (*Crown Copyright/Air Historical Branch image PRB-1-21020*)

Early Development of VTOL (Vertical Take-Off and Landing)

The Short SC.1 was the first British fixed-wing vertical take-off and landing (VTOL) jet aircraft. It was powered by a clever arrangement of five Rolls-Royce RB108 turbojets, four of which were used for vertical flight while the fifth was used to power the aircraft in conventional horizontal flight. The Short SC.1 had the distinction of being the first British fixed-wing VTOL aircraft and the first to transition between vertical and horizontal flight. This image depicts one of the Short SC.1 VTOL experimental aircraft displaying at the 1961 Farnborough Air Show. The aircraft was used to test the viability of vertical flight for a future RAF aircraft – the Harrier. (*Crown Copyright/Air Historical Branch image PRB-1-21665*)

Above: No. 92 Squadron – the Blue Diamonds – Sixteen-Aircraft Loop

For the 1961 Farnborough Air Show, the No. 92 Squadron display team, the Blue Diamonds, put together a sixteen-ship routine. Rehearsals for the expanded team began in July 1961, and this photograph was taken on 23 August during a press preview day at RAF Leconfield. Such was the demand for the principal display teams on Battle of Britain Day, and to accommodate as many of the open stations as possible, that the Blue Diamonds would give a display with their full complement at one or two locations before splitting into two still substantial aerobatic formations to display at other stations. At the Farnborough Air Show the following year, a decision was made to fly a twenty-three-aircraft formation loop by combining the sixteen Hunter F.6 aircraft of No. 92 Squadron along with the seven-ship formation of Lightning F.1 aircraft from No. 74 Squadron. (*Crown Copyright/Air Historical Branch image PRB-1- 21551*)

Opposite: Sir Frank Whittle

Frank Whittle was a serving flight lieutenant studying on a postgraduate year at Cambridge University when he ground-tested his first gas turbine engine on 12 April 1937. The engine had a single-stage centrifugal compressor coupled to a single-stage turbine. On 15 May 1941, the first flight by a British jet-propelled aircraft – the Gloster E28/39 – took place at RAF Cranwell. At the controls for the historic event was D. E. G. Sayer, Gloster's chief test pilot, and the aircraft flew for a total of 17 minutes. Air Commodore Sir Frank Whittle is pictured during a visit to the RAF College Cranwell in October 1962, during which he opened the College's new training wing, which had been named in his honour. (*Crown Copyright/Air Historical Branch image PRB-1-23970*)

THE WHITTLE W.1 GAS TURBINE ENGINE

AN ENGINE OF THIS TYPE INSTALLED IN THE GLOSTER E28/39 MADE THE FIRST JET-POWERED FLIGHT IN THIS COUNTRY AT CRANWELL ON THE 15th MAY, 1941.

THIS ENGINE, FROM WHICH THE 'DERWENT' WAS DEVELOPED TO POWER THE GLOSTER METEOR, ALSO PROVIDED THE STARTING POINT FOR UNITED STATES DEVELOPMENT IN JET PROPULSION.

The Winter of 1963

Residents of Simonsbath, on the edge of the Exmoor National Park, approach a Whirlwind HAR.10 of No. 230 Squadron (XP402/X) which has just landed with relief supplies in January of 1963. In what were believed to be the largest operations of their kind to have been undertaken by the RAF, helicopters from Nos 225 and 230 Squadrons at RAF Odiham and No. 22 Squadron at RAF Chivenor transported people stranded in remote areas while Transport Command Beverleys dropped cattle fodder to aid farmers. (*Crown Copyright/Air Historical Branch PRB-1-24459*)

Blue Steel Stand-Off Nuclear Missile

A Blue Steel stand-off nuclear missile is loaded from its storage trolley on to a transporter at RAF Scampton in February 1963. Blue Steel, built by Avro, was introduced into service by No. 617 Squadron in 1963. It carried a one megaton warhead and was used by two squadrons in Bomber Command – Nos 617 (Avro Vulcan B2) and 139 (Handley Page Victor B2). Capable of being launched some 100 miles from its target, the missile reduced the need for any deep penetration of enemy defences to carry out an attack. (*Crown Copyright/Air Historical Branch image PRB-1-24621*)

Above: **Ballistic Missile Early Warning System (BMEWS)**
In January 1964, the Ballistic Missile Early Warning Unit (BMEWU) at RAF Fylingdales, on the North Yorkshire Moors, became fully operational. RAF Fylingdales was the third BMEWU to become fully operational; its companion units operated by the United States Air Force were at Thule in Greenland and Clear in Alaska. Together they spread a blanket of radar beams around 3,000 miles across Europe and Asia to provide almost constant warning should ballistic missiles be launched against the UK or North America. In the event of the UK being threatened, Fylingdales would ensure sufficient warning for V force aircraft to take off before destruction on the ground. This was considered to be the worst situation, assuming the minimum warning period of 4 minutes to which Bomber Command alert procedures was geared. The BMEWU system was regarded as an effective deterrent to war, since it was a reminder to any potential attacker that the nations of the Free World would have time to get their own missiles and bombers on the way for retaliation before the aggressors' own missiles hit their target. (*Crown Copyright/Air Historical Branch image T-3559*)

Opposite: **English Electric Lightning**
The English Electric (later BAC) Lightning was the first single-seat fighter designed for the RAF to exceed the speed of sound in level flight, thus becoming the very first true British supersonic fighter, as earlier types – such as the Swift and Hunter – could only achieve this feat in a dive. After the prototype P.1A and P.1B aircraft were completely re-engineered and re-engined with a pair of Rolls-Royce Avon 200 engines, the true potential of the design could be achieved. The Lightning went on to achieve a maximum speed of Mach 2.1 (around 1,500 mph) at 36,000 feet although its initial rate of climb – at 20,000 ft/min. – was what made it stand out from its contemporaries. In this image, nine English Electric Lightning F.1A fighters of the No. 56 Squadron display team, the Firebirds, were photographed in 'Diamond Nine' formation in September 1963. This spectacular formation had originally been pioneered by No. 74 Squadron in 1961 and it became the main feature of the Firebirds display. It was achieved by combining two separate sections: the front five aircraft led by Squadron Leader Dave Seward and the box of four aircraft ('Green' section) led by Flt Lt John Curry. (*Crown Copyright/Air Historical Branch image T-4163*)

Yellowjacks

The RAF Gnat Aerobatic Team – the Yellowjacks – from No. 4 Flying Training School, RAF Valley, in July 1964. To ensure the RAF Valley team did not conflict with the official RAF team from Little Rissington – the Red Pelicans – it was decided to paint the Gnats in the traditional Flying Training Command high-visibility yellow colour scheme. There had been some suggestions during the work-up that the new colour scheme made the aircraft difficult to identify in less-than favourable weather conditions and for a brief period during July, one of the Gnats (XR992) had its fin painted black. The experiment proved inconclusive and was dropped after a few practice sorties. (*Crown Copyright/Air Historical Branch*)

Simons Bomb Hoist

Handley Page Victor B.1A XH645, of No. 57 Squadron, based at RAF Marham, is loaded with conventional 1,000 lb bombs at Tengah, Singapore, for a sortie over Borneo during operations in 1964. The ordnance is being loaded with the assistance of the Simons Bomb Hoist, seen here mounted onto the chassis of a Bedford truck, which accessed the bomb bay via a hatch on the aircraft's spine. The same equipment could be used to remove or fit the Valiant's wing fuel tanks. (*Crown Copyright/Air Historical Branch image T-5194*)

Above: First flight of the TSR-2

After overcoming many hurdles, the first TSR.2 prototype, XR219, finally made its maiden flight from the A&AEE facility at Boscombe Down during the afternoon of Sunday 27 September 1964 – some eighteen months later than planned. Even after five months of ground tests, there were still many issues – notably with the Bristol Olympus 320 engines – but permission to go ahead with the maiden flight within certain parameters (and with many internal systems not fitted) was given. It was also hoped that the flight would finally garner some political support in the light of a forthcoming general election with every chance of a change of government, something that, unfortunately, did not come to fruition. No further flights would be made before the end of the year. This view of XR219 was captured at around 10,000 ft, showing the aircraft in full landing configuration with undercarriage down, partly extended airbrakes (just behind the twin mainwheels), wing flaps in the fully deployed position and auxiliary air doors open. The first flight lasted for just 15 minutes before XR219 returned to Boscombe Down. The aircraft was flown by Roland Beamont, the BAC chief test pilot, and Donald Bowen, BAC's chief navigator. Afterwards, Beamont described the TSR.2 as 'a real winner, a very good aeroplane'. (*Crown Copyright/Air Historical Branch image PRB-1-28700*)

Opposite: Formation of a Permanent RAF Display Team

With the increasing sophistication and cost of fighter aircraft, as well as the considerable disruption to their units, the RAF decided to form the first permanent display team – known as the Royal Air Force Aerobatic Team (RAFAT) – administered by the Central Flying School (CFS) at Little Rissington. The advantages of a permanent team were seen at the time as numerous: to raise British and RAF prestige, as well as flying standards and morale within the services; to stimulate recruiting; and to publicise the merits of British aviation in the world marketplace. Looking back over the years, this final aspect has been carried out to considerable effect. The Red Arrows were presented to the media at Little Rissington on 6 May 1965 before they gave their first official display at the French National Air Meeting at Clermont Ferrand. The first opportunity for the UK public to see them was at the Biggin Hill Air Fair on 15 May 1965, where the seven Gnat aircraft put on a 15-minute display in front of a crowd of 40,000 people. (*Crown Copyright*)

Above: The RAF College

Originally established as a naval aviation training centre during the First World War, the Royal Air Force College was established as the world's first air academy on 1 November 1919, as the RAF (Cadet) College, under the Chief of the Air Staff, Sir Hugh Trenchard. In this image, taken in 1965, a pair of Jet Provost T.4 aircraft – serial numbers XP547/82 and XP566/81 – were photographed while flying over the RAF College at Cranwell. (*Crown Copyright/Air Historical Branch image T-5457*)

Opposite above: Univac 1107 Computer

The very first computer system installed for use by the RAF was the Univac 1107. When the installation of an electronic data processing system was first considered in 1957, the pay and personnel records of all RAF personnel were not even centralised. The centralisation of all of the pay and personnel information began on 1 July 1965 as 'No. 4 Division' and by the end of 1968, the computer had taken over the personnel and pay recording, along with the production of statistical information on all serving airmen and airwomen. (*Crown Copyright/Air Historical Branch image PRB-1-33888*)

Opposite below: The Queen's Flight

The King's Flight was officially created back in 1936 and became the Queen's Flight in 1953. Both the King's and Queen's Flight operated British-manufactured aircraft and flew them to all parts of the globe. On 1 April 1995, the Queen's Flight was merged with No. 32 Squadron to become No. 32 (The Royal) Squadron. This view depicts a typical Queen's Flight scene on the ramp at RAF Benson during the mid-1960s. Left to right are Whirlwind HCC.12 XR486, Heron C.4 XR391 and Andover C.2 XS789. (*Crown Copyright/Air Historical Branch image T-8065*)

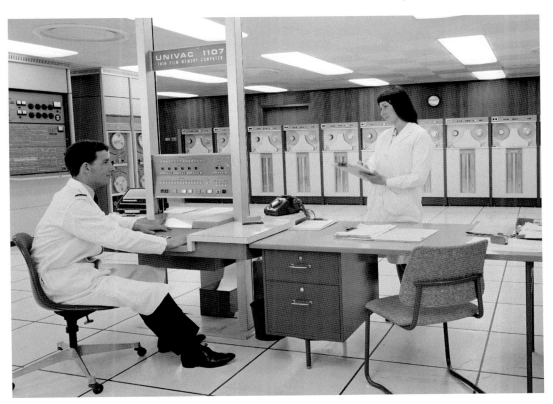

The Empire Test Pilots' School (ETPS)

Having been established at MoD Boscombe Down in 1943, the Empire Test Pilots' School was the very first of its type anywhere in the world, specialising in the training of test pilots and flight test engineers. It moved to RAF Cranfield in October 1945 and to the RAE at Farnborough in July 1947, before returning to Boscombe Down on 29 January 1968. Now the ETPS is run by the MoD defence contractor Qinetiq under a long-term agreement. This air-to-ground image taken at Boscombe Down in March 1967 shows the vast array of aircraft used by the Empire Test Pilots' School. Eighteen aircraft are pictured in this view. All aircraft operated by the ETPS were specifically chosen because of their handling characteristics, for use in teaching widely varied aspects of aircraft handling. The line-up on the left (and mirrored on the right) consists of a Chipmunk, Piston Provost, Dove, Canberra and Vickers Viscount; the centre line has the only Short SB.5 research aircraft (WG768), Lightning T.4, two single-seat and a pair of two-seat Hunters and a Twin Pioneer. Behind the Viscount at the far end of the right-hand line is a Westland Whirlwind helicopter. (*Crown Copyright/Air Historical Branch image PRB-1-36287*)

MRCA – Multi-Role Combat Aircraft

Known initially as the MRCA (Multi-Role Combat Aircraft) and designed and produced by the European consortium Panavia, consisting of British, German and Italian manufacturers, the variable-geometry aircraft was to become one of the most outstanding achievements of modern aeronautical engineering. The first British-manufactured Panavia MRCA aircraft – XX946, construction number P-02 – was photographed on 30 October 1974 during the aircraft's first flight from BAC Military Aircraft Division's Warton airfield. The aircraft was flown by Paul Millett, the Military Aircraft Division's chief test pilot, with Pietro Trevisan, Aeritalia's MRCA project pilot, in the second seat. The flight lasted an hour. The three-nation project was ultimately developed the design into the Tornado GR.1 fighter-bomber. (*Crown Copyright/Air Historical Branch image TN-1-7336-5*)

The RAF Regiment

The RAF Regiment is part of the RAF and functions as a specialist airfield defence corps. The RAF Regiment is trained in CBRN (chemical, biological, radiological and nuclear) defence. In this image, an RAF Regiment Rapier missile battery team, of No. 27 Squadron RAF Regiment, was photographed checking for incoming raiders during a station exercise at RAF Leuchars on 21 May 1976. (*Crown Copyright/Air Historical Branch image TN-1-7511-4*)

The Ejection Seat

The Martin-Baker Aircraft Company was formed in 1934, initially to produce aircraft. However, it soon started to investigate ejection seats, some four years ahead of companies in both Germany and Sweden. Martin-Baker concluded that an explosive-powered ejection seat would be the best solution and, after completing extensive studies on the human tolerances to such an upward acceleration, commenced trials. Bernard Lynch, a fitter with the company, volunteered to make the first experimental launch. On 24 July 1946, he made the very first 'live' ejection from a modified Gloster Meteor above Chalgrove Airfield in Oxfordshire. The very first use of an ejector seat occurred on 30 May 1949, when the Armstrong Whitworth test pilot – J. O. Lancaster – ejected from the AW42 experimental wing aircraft at 3,000 feet. Martin-Baker went on to develop the ejector seat and eventually developed a solution which lead to a 'zero-zero' capability – at zero height and zero speed. In this image, armourers refit one of the two ejection seats in a Hawk T.1 of No. 4 Flying Training School during a routine servicing at RAF Valley on 20 February 1978. (*Crown Copyright/Air Historical Branch image TN-1-7835-51*)

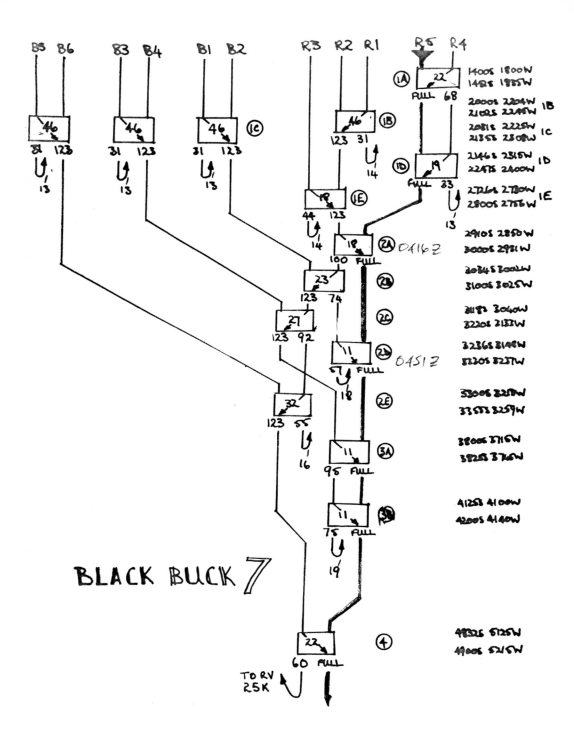

BLACK BUCK 7

78

Above: Humanitarian Relief

A widespread famine affected Ethiopia from 1983 to 1985. It was the worst famine to hit the country in a century and in the north of the country led to more than 400,000 deaths; in 1985 alone, close to eight million people became famine victims. On 23 October 1984, a BBC news crew were the first to document the famine, with Michael Buerk describing 'a biblical famine in the twentieth century' and 'the closest thing to hell on earth'. In January 1985, the RAF carried out the first airdrops from Hercules aircraft, delivering food to the starving people. Buerk's news piece was seen by Bob Geldof, who quickly organised the charity supergroup Band Aid. This image shows a Hercules C.1 XV215 of the Lyneham Tactical Wing, taking part in Operation Bushell, the international famine aid programme in Ethiopia, during January 1985. (*Crown Copyright/Air Historical Branch image TN-1-9752-38*)

Opposite: Operation Black Buck

Operations Black Buck 1 to Black Buck 7 were a series of extremely long-range ground attack missions flown by the RAF during the 1982 Falklands War using Vulcan bomber aircraft of the Waddington Wing comprising Nos 44, 50 and 101 Squadrons. The objectives of all missions were to attack Port Stanley airfield and its associated defences, denying the Argentinean Air Force use of it. The final mission in XM607 was led by Flight Lieutenant Martin Withers against Argentinean troop positions close to Stanley on 12 June, cratering the eastern end of the airfield and causing widespread damage to airfield stores and facilities. This image depicts the outbound fuel flow plan for the Black Buck 7 mission, flown on 12 June 1982, the final conventional bombing raid against Stanley on the Falkland Islands. The complexity of providing sufficient air-to-air refuelling capabilities from Victor tanker aircraft in order to permit a single Vulcan to achieve its objectives is obvious! (*Crown Copyright/Air Historical Branch image Falk-BlackBucc7*)

Above: NBC Protective Suits
Groundcrew from No. 5 Squadron equipped with NBC (Nuclear, Biological and Chemical Weapons) suits during Exercise Elder Forest at RAF Coningsby on 22 April 1988. Their Tornado F.3, serial number ZE761/CC, is being prepared for operations inside one of the base's HASs (Hardened Aircraft Shelters). (*Crown Copyright/Air Historical Branch image TN-2-294-28*)

Opposite above: Nimrod AEW.3
The British Aerospace Nimrod AEW.3 was intended to provide airborne radar cover for the air defence of the UK. It was designed to utilise an existing Nimrod airframe, then in use with the RAF as a maritime patrol aircraft, combined with a new radar system, computerisation and avionics package. The project proved to be hugely complex and expensive for the British Government; not the least of the challenges came in trying to integrate the new radar, computer and avionics into an existing Nimrod airframe. Despite almost ten years' development work, the project was eventually cancelled, with the RAF choosing to purchase Boeing E-3 Sentry aircraft to fulfil the AEW requirements. This image shows BAe Nimrod AEW.3 serial XZ286 during the flight test programme. (*Crown Copyright/ Air Historical Branch image AHB-MIS-SLIDE-NIM3-3*)

Opposite below: RAPTOR Camera System
The Reconnaissance Airborne Pod Tornado (RAPTOR) is a reconnaissance pod used by the RAF on its fleet of Tornado GR.4A aircraft. The RAPTOR is manufactured by the Goodrich Corporation and contains a DB-110 reconnaissance sensor, an image data recording system and an air-to-ground data link system. The sensor is electro-optical and infrared, allowing both day and night operations. The RAF procured eight RAPTOR units and two ground stations, and the equipment achieved its operational debut during Operation Telic, as part of the 2003 Iraq War. This image taken at Kandahar airfield depicts a Tornado GR.4 with the Raptor Camera System mounted underneath. The aircraft is being flown by personnel from No. 12 Squadron, based at RAF Lossiemouth. (*Crown Copyright/Air Historical Branch image DMOC-2011-007-116/LA Iggy Roberts*)

Above: Typhoon

The Eurofighter Typhoon was designed as an air-superiority fighter and is manufactured by a consortium consisting of Airbus, BAe Systems and Leonardo. The aircraft's development effectively began in 1983 with the Future European Fighter Aircraft programme, a multinational collaboration among the UK, Germany, France, Italy and Spain. A number of disagreements led France to leave the consortium and develop its own Dassault Rafale design. The maiden flight of the Eurofighter took place on 27 March 1994 with the first RAF deliveries being made to No. 11 Squadron on 29 March 2007 and being declared combat ready in the air-to-ground role by 1 July 2008. This image depicts a No. 17 Squadron Typhoon photographed over the North Sea on 25 September 2007 while equipped with a pair of air-to-air missiles along with six laser-guided bombs. (*Crown Copyright/Air Historical Branch image 07-889-UNCLASS-176(E)/Sgt Gary Morgan*)

Opposite: NVG (Night Vision Goggles)

Night Vision Goggles (NVG) are an optoelectronic device that allows images to be produced in levels of light approaching total darkness. The image produced is typically monochrome, although displayed in shades of green. This image shows Flight Lieutenant Mark Robertson, then a Harrier pilot with IV(AC) Squadron, part of the Joint Force Harrier based at RAF Cottesmore, wearing Night Vision Goggles (NVG). (*Crown Copyright/Air Historical Branch image return of the jedi/ COT-08-263-OUT-UNC-030/ Cpl Heidi Cox*)

Above: Harrier Operations Farewell Formation

The Harrier concept originated in the P.1127 Kestrel and was the first VTOL combat aircraft to enter regular squadron service with any air force in the world. Aside from the trainer versions, it also operated with the RAF as the GR.1, GR.3, GR.5, GR.7 and GR.9 variants. The first Harrier GR.1 was delivered to No. 1 Squadron at RAF Wittering in July 1969. Thanks to a development programme along with a series of upgrades, the Harrier remained in service with the RAF until 2010, although many still consider the type's withdrawal to have been premature and politically motivated. This image – taken on 15 December 2010 – features sixteen Harriers in a special formation to commemorate the type's last day of flying and features a number of aircraft painted in special commemorative colour schemes. (*Crown Copyright/Air Historical Branch image COT-10-865-UNCLASS-001/Cpl Al Crowe*)

Opposite above: Paveway Laser-Guided Bombs (LGBs)

The Paveway series of laser-guided bombs was developed by Texas Instruments, starting in 1964. The first test weapon, using a M117 bomb as the warhead, took place in April 1965. Various iterations of Paveway have since been developed and the RAF acquired Raytheon's advanced Paveway IV 500 lb (227 kg) bomb in 2008 and the munition has been in service ever since, having been used in a number of operations including the First Gulf War. This image shows a number of Paveway IV weapons having been loaded onto an RAF Tornado GR.4 aircraft at Gioia Del Colle AFB, Italy, while operating in support of UN Resolution 1973 on 28 March 2011. (*Crown Copyright/Air Historical Branch image EAW906-11-0009-UNC-005/Cpl Babbs Robinson*)

Opposite below: Detachment Artwork

It has become customary for various armed forces to create artwork at their deployed locations. This image shows the artwork created by members of the various squadrons deployed on 904 EA to Kandahar Airfield, Afghanistan. UK forces were deployed to Afghanistan and the Broader Middle East in support of the UN-authorised, NATO-led International Security Assistance Force (ISAF) mission, and as a part of the US-led Operation Enduring Freedom (OEF). UK operations in Afghanistan were being conducted under the name Operation Herrick, while the Broader Middle East falls under Operation Kipion. (*Crown Copyright/Air Historical Branch image AUAB-UNC-20131029-0166-007*)

Brimstone Anti-Radar Missile

Brimstone is an air-launched ground attack missile developed by MBDA (Matra/BAe Dynamics) for the RAF. Originally designed as a 'fire-and-forget' weapon for use against mass formations of enemy armour, experience gained from operations in Afghanistan led to the addition of laser-guidance in the dual-mode Brimstone missile. Three Brimstone missiles are usually carried on a launcher that occupies a single weapons station, allowing a single aircraft to carry many missiles, and the dual-mode weapon has been used extensively in both Afghanistan and Libya. This is another image from Gioia Del Colle AFB, Italy, while the RAF was operating in support of UN Resolution 1973 on 28 March 2011 and features an RAF Tornado GR.4 aircraft with a launcher containing three Brimstone anti-radar missiles located on the underside of the fuselage along with a Litening Pod. (*Crown Copyright/Air Historical Branch image EAW906-11-0009-UNC-0197/Cpl Babbs Robinson*)

Rubb Hangar

Rubb Building Systems manufactures special buildings and shelters, often for specialist temporary use. When RAF Northolt hosted Typhoon fighters from RAF Coningsby for a nine-day military exercise ahead of the then forthcoming 2012 Olympic Games in London, Rubb hangars were used to house the aircraft. Exercise Olympic Guardian ran from 2 May to 9 May and built upon the RAF's existing defence of UK airspace to protect from potential threats during the Olympic Games. (*Crown Copyright/Air Historical Branch image NHT-UNCLASS-2012-05-04-0124-0289*)

Hardened Aircraft Shelter (HAS)

Something of a relic from the Cold War, a hardened aircraft shelter (HAS) is a reinforced hangar to house and protect military aircraft from enemy attack. They were first installed at bases on RAF Germany stations in the 1970s and were subsequently built at a number of RAF fighter stations in the UK. This image, taken at RAF Coningsby on 17 January 2013, shows a HAS in use during rather wintry conditions at the Lincolnshire base. (*Crown Copyright/Air Historical Branch image CON-UNCLASS-20130117-0044-15/Senior Aircraftsman Daniel Herrick*)

RAF Regiment Wolfhound

No. 34 Squadron from Royal Air Force Leeming and No. 15 Squadron from Royal Air Force Honington on a training exercise at Warcop Ranges for the build-up to Operation Herrick 20, Afghanistan, in April 2014. The vehicle is a Wolfhound, a six-wheeled variant of the acclaimed Mastiff, which provides troops with increased protection as they support missions in high-threat areas. This heavy armoured truck is part of the Tactical Support Vehicles (TSV) group along with the Husky and the Coyote. The TSV fleet is used to accompany front line patrols and carry essential combat supplies such as water and ammunition. It provides a highly protected load-carrying vehicle to carry out a variety of tasks such as moving bulky stores for use in the construction of forward bases and also as a gun tractor and gun limber for the Royal Artillery's 105 mm light gun. Wolfhound is armed with a 7.62 GPMG self-defence weapon and the normal fit of radio and electronic equipment. (*Crown Copyright/Air Historical Branch image 'May the force be with you'/Cpl Babbs Robinson*)

QRA – 24/7, 365 Days a Year

QRA Typhoon aircraft and their pilots provide a UK air defence capability 24 hours a day, 365 days a year from RAF stations at both Lossiemouth and Coningsby and are supported by personnel from across the RAF including Airspace Battle Managers, Air Traffic Controllers and the squadron engineers who, like the pilots, take shifts to ensure QRA aircraft are permanently ready to fly. Their purpose is to provide an air defence capability ready to detect, deter and if necessary destroy any aircraft intending to attack any target within the UK. However, QRA aircraft are also 'scrambled' in support of NATO to intercept and escort Russian long-range aviation aircraft, such as the Tu-95 Bear, whenever they are flying within the NATO air policing areas that surround the UK. This image depicts a Russian Bear aircraft being escorted by an RAF Quick Reaction Alert (QRA) Typhoon, ZK317/ES of No. 6 Squadron, during an intercept in September 2014. (*Crown Copyright/Air Historical Branch image 45158137*)

Storm Shadow

Storm Shadow is a low-observable air-launched cruise missile manufactured by MBDA. Storm Shadow entered RAF service in late 2001 and was used during the First Gulf War in 2003 by No. 617 Squadron. It was later used in the NATO intervention of the Libyan civil war and then against an ISIS bunker in Iraq on 26 June 2016. This image shows a No. 617 Squadron Tornado GR.4, ZA462/AJ-P, photographed while flying from RAF Lossiemouth, equipped with two Storm Shadow weapons mounted in the underside of the fuselage. (*Crown Copyright/Air Historical Branch image GL-031341*)

RPAS (Remotely Piloted Air Systems)

Remotely Piloted Air Systems (RPAS) have seen an exponential growth in the last twenty years. The ability to operate a quiet, stealthy aircraft, with a very long range and effectively flown by an 'operator' at a remote ground location, has been used operationally to good effect. The growth in UCAV (Unmanned Combat Aerial Vehicles) is expected to continue. This image shows a No. 39 Squadron Reaper, ZZ203, landing after a sortie in Afghanistan. (*Crown Copyright/Air Historical Branch image is-5155-hr/Cpl Andy Benson*)

F-35B Lightning II
The Lockheed Martin F-35 Lightning II is a family of single-seat, single-engine multirole fighter aircraft under development to perform ground attack, reconnaissance, and air defence missions with stealth capability. It was selected for the UK's Joint Combat Aircraft requirement in 2001 and will become the main component of the RAF's manned strike capability. Delivery of the first F-35B was made to the RAF on 19 July 2012 at Fort Worth, for trials by the RAF and Royal Navy. Pictured is an RAF F-35B flying over RAF Marham. The image was taken on an historic day for the UK as the future of the Royal Navy and Royal Air Force combat air fleets, the F-35B Lightning II, flew over their prospective 'homes' – Rosyth and RAF Marham in Norfolk. The fifth generation F-35B jets are the most advanced aircraft ever built for the UK and will be operated initially by No. 617 Squadron and later by No. 809 Naval Air Squadron. (*Crown Copyright/Air Historical Branch image 45162426*)

On this, the centenary of its formation, I send my heartfelt congratulations to the Royal Air Force at home and overseas, and to all of its families and loved ones.

The anniversary of the world's first independent Air Force is of great significance, and it is fitting to pay tribute to the tenacity, skill and sacrifice of the men and women who have served within its ranks over the last century, and who have defended our freedom so gallantly.

Through its enduring focus on professionalism, excellence and innovation, the Royal Air Force stands as a shining example of inspiration around the World today and for the next generations.

May the glory and honour that all ranks have bestowed on the Royal Air Force light its pathway to the future, guarding our skies and reaching for the stars.

Per Ardua ad Astra.

ELIZABETH R.

A letter From HM the Queen Congratulating the RAF Upon Reaching its Centenary
(*Crown Copyright/Air Historical Branch image NHT-Official-2018-02-12-027-013*)